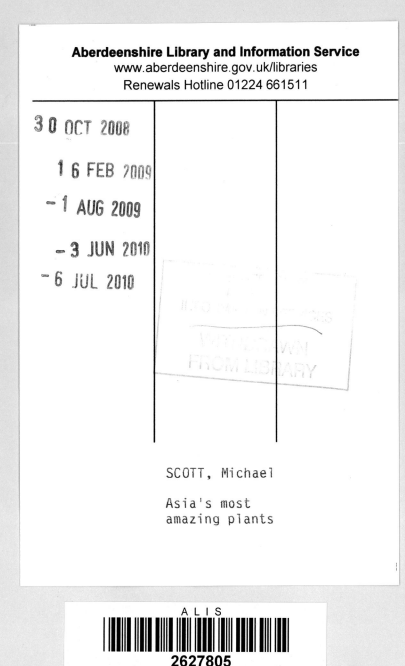

Plant Top Tens

Asia's Most Amazing Plants

www.raintreepublishers.co.uk
Visit our website to find out more information about Raintree Books.

To order:
☎ Phone 44 (0) 1865 888112
📄 Send a fax to 44 (0) 1865 314091
💻 Visit the Raintree Bookshop at **www.raintreepublishers.co.uk** to browse our catalogue and order online

First published in Great Britain by Raintree, Halley Court, Jordan Hill, Oxford OX2 8EJ, part of Pearson Education.
Raintree is a registered trademark of Pearson Education Ltd.

Produced for Raintree by Calcium

Editorial: Kate deVilliers and Sarah Eason
Design: Victoria Bevan and Paul Myerscough
Illustrations: Geoff Ward
Picture Research: Maria Joannou
Production: Victoria Fitzgerald

Originated by Modern Age
Printed in China by South China Printing Company

ISBN 978 1 4062 0968 6
12 11 10 09 08
10 9 8 7 6 5 4 3 2 1

British Library Cataloguing in Publication Data
Scott, Michael and Royston, Angela
  Asia. - (Plant top tens)
  581.9'5
A full catalogue record for this book is available from the British Library.

Acknowledgements
The authors and publisher are grateful to the following for permission to reproduce copyright material: ©Alamy Images p. 12 (Dennis Frates); ©Corbis p. 8 (Frans Lanting); ©Dreamstime pp. 14 (Kuan Chong Ng), 17, 18 (Rewat Wannasuk); ©FLPA pp. 4, 21 (Frans Lanting), 10 (Nicholas and Sherry Lu Aldridge); ©Istockphoto pp. 15, 19, 22; ©NHPA pp. 6 (Khalid Ghani), 20 (Nick Garbutt); ©Jay Pfahl p. 27; ©Photolibrary pp. 9 (David Kirkland), 13 (Garden Picture Library/Michele Lamontagne), 23 (Fresh Food Images); ©Shutterstock pp. 7 (Ng Wei Keong), 16 (Tito Wong), 24, 25; ©Still Pictures p. 11 (Mustafiz Mamun/Majority World); ©Wikipedia p. 26 (Peter Bourne).

Cover photograph of a rafflesia, reproduced with permission of Photolibrary/Oxford Scientific Films/ David Cayless.

Every effort has been made to contact copyright holders of any material reproduced in this book. Any omissions will be rectified in subsequent printings if notice is given to the publishers.

Contents

Some words are printed in bold, **like this**. You can find out what they mean on page 31 in the Glossary.

Asia

Asia stretches from the frozen **Arctic** Ocean in the north to the hot **tropics** in the south. Asia has many types of **habitat**. These include **tropical rainforests, deserts,** and mountains. A habitat includes the plants and animals that live in a place. Tropical rainforests are warm and wet all year round. Millions of different types of plant grow here.

Asian rainforests

Asia has two kinds of **rainforest**. In a true rainforest, it rains almost every day and the trees have leaves all year round. In a **monsoon rainforest**, it is dry for part of the year. Then most of the trees lose their leaves.

Asia has many tropical rainforests.

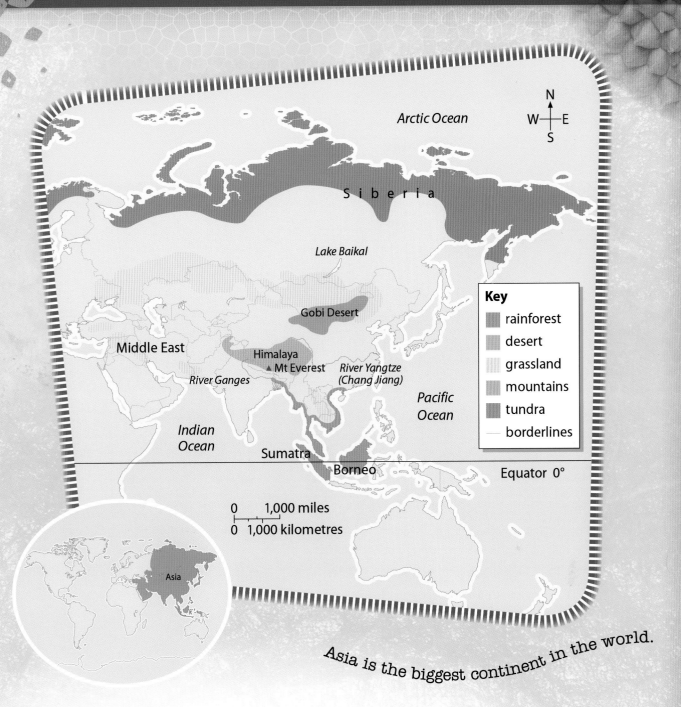

Asia is the biggest continent in the world.

Near the Arctic Ocean the land is frozen in winter and is a wet **bog** in summer. Only a few kinds of plant can grow here. Asia has the highest mountains in the world. High mountain slopes are covered with snow for most of the year. Here, also, few plants can grow.

Teak

Teak is a huge tree that grows in monsoon rainforests. The tree grows so tall because the forests are hot and often wet. It rains heavily for most of the year. It is dry for only three to six months. Teak trees save water during the dry season by dropping their leaves. This stops them losing water through tiny holes in the leaves.

Teak trees need plenty of space. They never grow close together.

Tree king

Teak is called "the king of woods" because it is so valuable. It is very hard and it contains a strong, oily liquid called **resin**. The resin repels insects and other animals that might bore into it. The resin also stops the wood from rotting. For these reasons, teak wood is often used for the decks and masts of boats.

Teak trees are specially grown to be used to make furniture and many other things.

TEAK

HEIGHT:
UP TO 46 METRES (150 FEET)

LIFESPAN:
200 YEARS OR MORE

HABITAT:
MONSOON RAINFORESTS

THAT'S AMAZING!
THE SHIP RMS *TITANIC* SANK NEARLY 100 YEARS AGO. ITS TEAK DECKS HAVE LAIN ON THE BOTTOM OF THE SEA SINCE THEN. THEY STILL HAVE NOT ROTTED!

where teak trees are found

Asia

Pacific Ocean

Indian Ocean

Rafflesia

Rafflesia (say "raff-lees-ee-a") is the largest flower in the world. It is also the smelliest. Its horrible smell attracts flies, which mistake it for rotting meat. The flies take **pollen** from one flower to another. The flowers use the pollen to make **seeds**. When the seeds are ripe, they can grow into new plants.

RAFFLESIA

WIDTH:
THE FLOWER IS UP TO 1 METRE (40 INCHES) ACROSS

LIFESPAN:
FLOWERS LAST 5–7 DAYS AND THE PLANT LIVES LESS THAN A YEAR

HABITAT:
RAINFORESTS

THAT'S AMAZING!
RAFFLESIA FLOWERS WEIGH UP TO 11 KILOGRAMS (24 LBS). THAT IS AS HEAVY AS 36 HARDBACK BOOKS THE SIZE OF THIS ONE.

where rafflesias are found

Asia

Pacific Ocean

Indian Ocean

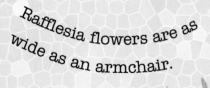

Rafflesia flowers are as wide as an armchair.

Vine parasite

Rafflesias grow on the **stems** of other **vines**. They grow in rainforests, where there are lots of vines for them to grow on. They have no leaves and almost no stem of their own. Their roots grow into the stem of the vine and steal the vine's sap. The sap contains sugar and water. Plants that steal another plant's sap are called **parasites**.

The rafflesia's smell attracts insects. So do its red petals.

Mangrove

Mangrove trees grow along the coast. The soil here is covered with salt water twice a day. Salt water kills most plants. The mangrove can only live here because its roots stop some of the salt getting into the plant. The roots grow from the trunk down into the mud. They prop up the tree and stop it getting washed away by the waves.

The roots of mangrove trees are often covered with salty sea water.

Roots
The roots of most plants anchor them in the soil. Roots take in water and **nutrients** from the soil.

Deer and other animals live on the new land that forms around the roots of mangrove trees.

Making new land

Mangroves often grow at the mouths of rivers. The tangled roots catch mud swept down by the river. The mud hardens among the roots. It forms new land just above the level of the sea.

where mangroves are found

Asia

Pacific Ocean

Indian Ocean

Himalayan poppy

Himalayan poppies grow on rocky slopes and cliffs high in the Himalaya Mountains. Up here the summer is short, cold, and wet. In winter the ground is covered with snow. Most plants here grow close to the ground to avoid the strong winter winds. Himalayan poppies, however, grow as tall as a 12-year-old child.

The flower of a Himalayan poppy is up to 8 centimetres (3 inches) across.

HIMALAYAN POPPY

HEIGHT:
UP TO 1.5 METRES (5 FEET)

LIFESPAN:
A FEW YEARS (SOMETIMES JUST ONE YEAR)

HABITAT:
HIGH MOUNTAIN SLOPES

THAT'S AMAZING!
A POPPY'S SEED POD HAS A HOLE AT THE TIP. THE WIND SHAKES THE SEEDS FROM THE POD.

where Himalayan poppies are found

Asia

Pacific Ocean

Indian Ocean

Himalayan poppies are rare in the wild, but they are grown in gardens in many parts of the world.

Staying alive

When a Himalayan poppy has flowered, the plant dies but the thick root stays alive. It lies buried in the ground, sheltered from the wind. In winter the snow acts like a blanket. It helps to keep the root alive. When the snow melts, the root sprouts again and grows a new stem and flowers.

Durian

The durian plant has a big fruit that is shaped like a rugby ball. The fruit tastes delicious but it smells awful, like sweaty socks! The more ripe the fruit is, the more it smells. Many animals love this smell. Elephants, deer, orangutans, and tigers all eat durian fruit.

Spreading seeds

Seeds do not grow well if they fall on to the shaded ground below the parent tree. They grow better in fresh ground, far from the parent tree.

The fruits of the durian tree are eaten by many people in South-East Asia.

HEIGHT:
UP TO 40 METRES
(130 FEET)

LIFESPAN:
MANY YEARS

HABITAT:
TROPICAL RAINFORESTS

THAT'S AMAZING!
DURIAN FRUITS ARE SO SMELLY, SOME AIRLINES BAN PASSENGERS FROM TAKING THEM ON THEIR AIRCRAFT.

where durians are found

Asia

Pacific Ocean

Indian Ocean

Durian fruits are very healthy to eat, but you have to hold your nose!

Spiny plant

Durians grow in tropical rainforests. Many insects and other small animals live here. The fruit is covered with sharp spines. They protect it from being eaten by small animals. Small animals would nibble and damage the fruit without swallowing the seeds. Large animals eat the whole fruit. The seeds pass through their bodies and drop on to new ground.

Sacred lotus

The **sacred** lotus grows in still water. Its leaves are as big as umbrellas! It can grow so big because the water is always calm. A sacred lotus grows from a thick underground stem called a **rhizome**. The stalk of the leaf grows from the rhizome right up out of the water. Then it opens out into a large leaf.

The sacred lotus's huge leaves and flowers open above the surface of the water.

Flower of the gods

The flower grows up from the rhizome, too. The flower is so beautiful that many people in South-East Asia consider it to be sacred. This means that it is connected with the gods. People eat almost every part of the plant. The leaf stalks are used in salads. The rhizome is made into chips, and even into candied sweets.

The centre of a sacred lotus flower looks a bit like the spout of a watering can.

Bamboo

Bamboo is a type of grass, but it grows as tall as a tree. It can grow up to 90 centimetres (3 feet) a day. It is the fastest-growing flowering plant in the world. There are many different types of bamboo. Bamboo is used to make many things, such as chopsticks, baskets, mats, and boats.

Bamboo can grow as tall as a 12-storey building. The stems look like wood, but they are not wood.

BAMBOO

HEIGHT:
UP TO 40 METRES (130 FEET)

LIFESPAN:
OVER 120 YEARS FOR SOME TYPES

HABITAT:
OPEN GRASSLAND AND WOODLAND

THAT'S AMAZING!
SOME TYPES OF BAMBOO GROW FOR ABOUT 120 YEARS BEFORE THEY FLOWER ONCE, THEN THEY DIE.

where bamboo is found

Asia

Pacific Ocean

Indian Ocean

Bamboo shoots are almost the only food that giant pandas eat.

Panda food

Bamboo plants often grow close together to form bamboo forests. These forests provide food for many animals, including giant pandas. Bamboo forests trap water and help to keep the land and air healthy. Even so, many bamboo forests have been cut down to make way for farmland, roads, and cities.

Pitcher plant

A pitcher plant has leaves that grow into the shape of a cup, called a pitcher. The pitcher fills with rainwater. The biggest pitchers hold up to 2 litres (4 pints) of water. Insects drown in the water and the plant slowly eats them! The plant grows in **marshes** where the soil is poor, and on rainforest trees. The plant gets the extra food it needs by slowly eating the rotting insects.

Pitcher plants can grow only in places that are wet all the time.

Sugary juice

The plant produces a sugary juice inside the pitcher. The juice is called nectar. Insects climb into the pitcher to get the nectar, but they cannot climb out again. The walls are too slippery. Instead, they drown in the water. The plant makes chemicals called **enzymes**. These enzymes break down the dead insects so that the plant can take in their nutrients.

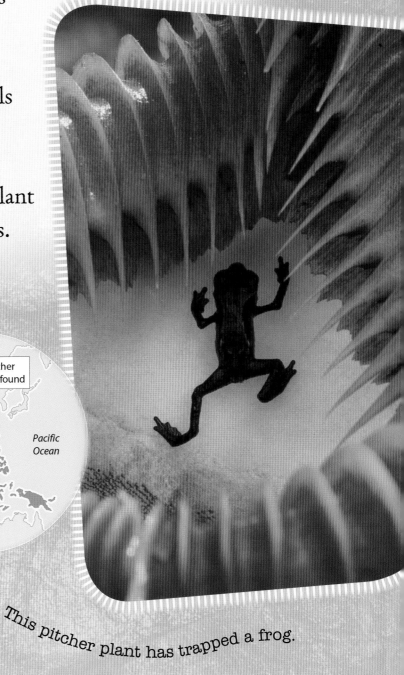

This pitcher plant has trapped a frog.

PITCHER PLANT

HEIGHT:
UP TO 50 CENTIMETRES
(20 INCHES)

LIFESPAN:
SEVERAL YEARS

HABITAT:
TROPICAL RAINFORESTS,
BOGS, AND MARSHES

THAT'S AMAZING!
THE LARGEST PITCHER
PLANTS HAVE EVEN TRAPPED
AND KILLED RATS.

where pitcher plants are found

Asia

Pacific
Ocean

Indian
Ocean

Coconut palm

A coconut palm uses the sea to spread its seeds. When a ripe coconut falls on to the beach, the waves wash it out to sea. Although a coconut is heavy, it has a thick, hairy coat that traps air. The air allows it to float. It floats until it is washed up on another beach.

Coconut palms grow on tropical beaches.

where coconut palms are found

Asia

Pacific Ocean

Indian Ocean

The best way to collect coconuts is to climb the tree and pick them!

Seeds

A seed contains the **bud** of a new plant. The bud is surrounded by a store of food. The bud feeds on the store until its roots and leaves have grown.

Tiny seeds

Under the hairy coat is a tough shell. It surrounds the juicy, white flesh. In the centre of the coconut is a hollow space with some coconut "milk". Inside the flesh is a tiny seed. The flesh and the milk feed the seed, and a new coconut palm begins to grow in the sand.

Bog moss

Bog mosses are more amazing than they look. They have no flowers or fruits. They also have no roots and no way of storing water. This means they can only grow in very wet places. The plants grow very close together in a tight cushion. The cushion soaks up water like a sponge. So bog mosses make their own wet bogs!

Bog moss has leaves and produces a special type of seed called a spore.

Peat can be burned as a fuel, like coal.

BOG MOSS

HEIGHT:
UP TO 10 CENTIMETRES
(4 INCHES)

LIFESPAN:
A FEW YEARS

HABITAT:
BOGS

THAT'S AMAZING!
THE BODIES OF PEOPLE WHO FELL INTO PEAT BOGS HUNDREDS OF YEARS AGO HAVE BEEN PERFECTLY PRESERVED. EVEN THE FOOD IN THEIR STOMACHS IS STILL THERE.

Asia

where bog mosses are found

Pacific Ocean

Indian Ocean

Bog pickle

When bog mosses die, they do not rot away completely. When they begin to rot, they produce an **acid**. The acid pickles living things that fall into it. The pickled remains of the bog and other plants and animals make peat. **Peat** bogs made by bog mosses cover about one seventh of the land in Indonesia.

Plants in danger

Some plants in Asia are in danger of dying out and becoming **extinct**. A plant or animal is extinct when there are none of them still alive. Plants become extinct for different reasons. Sometimes their habitat is destroyed. Sometimes the plants themselves are destroyed.

Himalayan elm trees are in danger because local people cut off their branches. They feed the leaves to their cattle, sheep, and goats.

Botanical gardens

Botanists are scientists who study plants. Many countries have **botanical gardens**. Here botanists grow plants that are in danger of becoming extinct, to preserve them.

This Himalayan elm has been grown in Brighton.

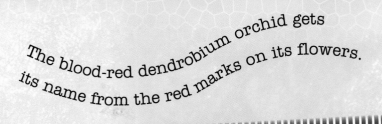
The blood-red dendrobium orchid gets its name from the red marks on its flowers.

Blood-red dendrobium orchids grow in forests in Thailand. The beautiful flowers last a long time. The plants are in danger because local people pick them to sell. These flowers are also grown by gardeners, so they will not die out completely.

Plant facts and figures

There are millions of different kinds of plants growing all over the world. The place where a plant lives is called its habitat. Plants have special features, such as flowers, leaves, and stems. These features allow plants to survive in their habitats. Which plant do you think is the most amazing?

TEAK

HEIGHT:
UP TO 46 METRES
(150 FEET)

LIFESPAN:
200 YEARS OR MORE

HABITAT:
MONSOON RAINFORESTS

THAT'S AMAZING!
THE SHIP RMS *TITANIC* SANK NEARLY 100 YEARS AGO. ITS TEAK DECKS HAVE LAIN ON THE BOTTOM OF THE SEA SINCE THEN. THEY STILL HAVE NOT ROTTED!

RAFFLESIA

WIDTH:
THE FLOWER IS UP TO 1 METRE (40 INCHES) ACROSS

LIFESPAN:
FLOWERS LAST 5–7 DAYS AND THE PLANT LIVES LESS THAN A YEAR

HABITAT:
RAINFORESTS

THAT'S AMAZING!
RAFFLESIA FLOWERS WEIGH UP TO 11 KILOGRAMS (24 LBS). THAT IS AS HEAVY AS 36 HARDBACK BOOKS THE SIZE OF THIS ONE.

MANGROVE

HEIGHT:
UP TO 25 METRES (82 FEET)

LIFESPAN:
PROBABLY 30–40 YEARS

HABITAT:
TROPICAL FORESTS ON THE COAST

THAT'S AMAZING!
MANGROVES HAVE EXTRA ROOTS THAT STICK OUT OF THE SEA LIKE SNORKELS. THEY TAKE IN OXYGEN FROM THE AIR TO KEEP THE PLANT ALIVE.

HIMALAYAN POPPY

HEIGHT:
UP TO 1.5 METRES (5 FEET)

LIFESPAN:
A FEW YEARS (SOMETIMES JUST ONE YEAR)

HABITAT:
HIGH MOUNTAIN SLOPES

THAT'S AMAZING!
A POPPY'S SEED POD HAS A HOLE AT THE TIP. THE WIND SHAKES THE SEEDS FROM THE POD.

DURIAN

HEIGHT:
UP TO 40 METRES
(130 FEET)

LIFESPAN:
MANY YEARS

HABITAT:
TROPICAL RAINFORESTS

THAT'S AMAZING!
DURIAN FRUITS ARE SO
SMELLY, SOME AIRLINES
BAN PASSENGERS FROM
TAKING THEM ON
THEIR AIRCRAFT.

SACRED LOTUS

WIDTH OF LEAVES:
UP TO 90 CENTIMETRES
(3 FEET)

LIFESPAN:
PROBABLY SEVERAL YEARS

HABITAT:
POOLS, MARSHES,
AND FLOODED FIELDS

THAT'S AMAZING!
A SACRED LOTUS SEED
WAS FOUND IN THE SOIL
OF AN ANCIENT LAKE IN
CHINA. ALTHOUGH THE
SEED WAS MORE THAN
1,000 YEARS OLD,
IT FLOWERED.

BAMBOO

HEIGHT:
UP TO 40 METRES
(130 FEET)

LIFESPAN:
OVER 120 YEARS FOR
SOME TYPES

HABITAT:
OPEN GRASSLAND AND
WOODLAND

THAT'S AMAZING!
SOME TYPES OF BAMBOO
GROW FOR ABOUT 120
YEARS BEFORE THEY
FLOWER ONCE, THEN
THEY DIE.

PITCHER PLANT

HEIGHT:
UP TO 50 CENTIMETRES
(20 INCHES)

LIFESPAN:
SEVERAL YEARS

HABITAT:
TROPICAL RAINFORESTS,
BOGS, AND MARSHES

THAT'S AMAZING!
THE LARGEST
PITCHER PLANTS HAVE
EVEN TRAPPED AND
KILLED RATS.

COCONUT PALM

HEIGHT:
UP TO 30 METRES

LIFESPAN:
80 YEARS OR MORE

HABITAT:
TROPICAL BEACHES
AND COASTS

THAT'S AMAZING!
SOME MONKEYS ARE
TRAINED TO COLLECT
COCONUTS. THEY CLIMB
THE TREES AND THROW
THE COCONUTS DOWN
TO THE PEOPLE BELOW.

BOG MOSS

HEIGHT:
UP TO 10 CENTIMETRES
(4 INCHES)

LIFESPAN:
A FEW YEARS

HABITAT:
BOGS

THAT'S AMAZING!
THE BODIES OF PEOPLE
WHO FELL INTO PEAT
BOGS HUNDREDS OF
YEARS AGO HAVE BEEN
PERFECTLY PRESERVED.
EVEN THE FOOD IN THEIR
STOMACHS IS STILL THERE.

Find out more

Books to read

Animals and Plants, Andrew Langley (Oxford University Press, 2002)

Plant Life Cycles, Anita Ganeri (Heinemann Library, 2006)

Plants and Planteaters (Secrets of the Rainforest), Michael Chinery (Crabtree Publishing Company, 2000)

Plants and the Environment, Jennifer Boothroyd (Lerner Publishing Group, 2007)

Plants that Eat Animals, Allan Fowler (Children's Press, 2001)

The Power of Plants, Claire Lewellyn (Oxford University Press, 2005)

The World's Largest Plants, Susan Blackaby (Picture Window Books, 2005)

Websites

www.bambooliving.com/PDF.cfm/BambooGrowing.pdf
Find out about bamboo and how it is used.

www.kidsgeo.com/geography-for-kids/0153-biosphere.php
Learn more about weather, habitats, and how plants survive in them.

www.mbgnet.net/bioplants/adapt.html
Discover how plants adapt to different habitats, including deserts, grasslands, tropical rainforests, temperate forests, tundra, and water.

www.plantcultures.org
Find out about plants from all over the world at Kew Gardens' website.

Glossary

acid sour liquid

Arctic area surrounding the North Pole

bog soft, wet ground

botanical garden garden where different kinds of plant are specially grown and studied

bud the beginning of a new plant, leaf, or flower

desert place that gets very little rain and has few plants

enzyme chemical that breaks down food

extinct no longer in existence

habitat place where particular kinds of plant grow and where particular animals live

maize plant that produces sweetcorn

marsh land that is partly covered by shallow water

monsoon rainforest forest that grows in places that get heavy rain for part of the year

nutrient part of food that is needed for health

oats plant that produces seeds that are made into food

parasite living thing that takes the food it needs from another living thing

peat substance made from the pickled remains of bog mosses and other plants and animals

pollen dust made by flowers

rainforest forest where it rains almost every day

resin oily liquid produced by some plants and trees

rhizome thick stem that grows under ground

sacred connected with God or with gods

seed part of a plant or tree that can grow into a new plant or tree

stem part of a plant on which leaves or a flower grows

tropical rainforest rainforest that grows near the Equator, where it is hot all year

tropics hot areas of the world on each side of the Equator

vine plant that grows along the ground or up a wall or up the stem of another plant

Index